# free from ocd

a workbook for
teens with **obsessive-
compulsive disorder**

TIMOTHY A. SISEMORE, PH.D.

Instant Help Books
A Division of New Harbinger Publications, Inc.

Distributed in Canada by Raincoast Books

Copyright © 2010 by Timothy A. Sisemore
              Instant Help Books
              A Division of New Harbinger Publications, Inc.
              5674 Shattuck Avenue
              Oakland, CA 94609
              www.newharbinger.com

Cover design by Amy Shoup

Printed in the United States of America

Library of Congress Cataloging-in-Publication Data

Sisemore, Timothy A.
  Free from OCD : a workbook for teens with obsessive-compulsive disorder / Timothy A. Sisemore.
    p. cm.
  ISBN 978-1-57224-848-9
  1. Obsessive-compulsive disorder in adolescence--Treatment. 2. Obsessive-compulsive disorder in adolescence--Popular works. I. Title.
  RJ506.O25S57 2010
  618.92'85227--dc22
                2010019138

18    17    16

10   9   8   7   6   5   4

# contents

# ✱ contents

# A Letter to Teens

Dear Friend,

From the fact that you picked up this workbook, I'd guess that you have faced some stubborn, troubling thoughts or some irritating, strong urges to repeat certain behaviors. You're certainly not alone. Many young people wrestle with similar problems, varying from some that are pretty mild to those that are so severe that they change almost every aspect of life. Most teenagers who have obsessions and compulsions keep them to themselves as best they can. They might confide in a parent, friend, or teacher, but for the most part they find the symptoms either embarrassing or fear getting teased about them. That's understandable—being young is hard enough without having to deal with obsessions and compulsions.

I believe that you can beat these problems, or at least make them a lot easier to deal with, if you faithfully work through this book. I know that the idea of a workbook may put you off, but it's the "work" that will make you better—not just reading. In fact, I think that the time you spend doing these activities will easily be made up by your spending less time dealing with stubborn thoughts and rituals.

These thoughts and rituals are part of a full-blown problem called obsessive-compulsive disorder (OCD). The primary symptoms are obsessions, or thoughts that occur over and over, which are usually worries about something bad happening. We'll be calling them "stuck thoughts" to stress that they don't have to be symptoms, just irritating problems. Compulsions are the almost irresistible impulses to do certain things over and over. They are often used to ease obsessions. We'll be calling these "rituals" in the pages ahead. But I don't want you to focus on whether or not you "officially" have OCD. Rather, if you have stuck thoughts and/or rituals, these activities should help. You may do them completely on your own or have a parent or friend help keep you going when the activities challenge you a bit. Either way, your efforts will help you regain control of your life, for stuck thoughts and rituals want control of your life, and they shouldn't have it.

So congratulations on taking the first step to beating these thoughts and rituals—admitting that these things are bothering you—and on picking up a book to help you do something about it.

I wish you the best as you break free from OCD.

Tim Sisemore

# A Letter to Parents or Caregivers

Dear Caring Adult,

Teens with obsessions and compulsions are usually not "bad" kids and so their anxiety and frustration are often overlooked. By being concerned enough about a teen in your life to look into this workbook, you've taken a step to help the young person you care about.

Teens vary in how open they are about obsessive-compulsive disorder (OCD), for it's a pain to feel controlled by these symptoms at a time of life when teens are trying to develop more freedom. But beating the symptoms of OCD can be very freeing (thus the title of the book) and can help teens move on into adulthood. Moreover, beating something as challenging as obsessions and compulsions can boost teens' self-confidence as they face challenges in the future.

Teens also vary in how much they'll want adults to be involved in their completion of this workbook. I suggest giving your teen that choice. You can serve as encourager and accountability partner, but only if the teen is receptive to that. You also can help if your teen gets stuck in obsessions or compulsions without being aware of it—again, only if he or she is open to that. If not, you may be seen as nagging or interfering. The bulk of the work in beating these symptoms is for your teen, not you. You might just ask what role your young person wants you to take, and stick to it.

The techniques in the book are built on scientifically supported strategies for counseling. I've turned them into activities so that many teens will be able to make progress without counseling. However, OCD can be stubborn and counseling often is necessary. These activities can also be part of such counseling. While medication can be helpful as well, I suggest at least giving the workbook and counseling chances first unless your teen is suffering so much that it is compromising a normal life.

I know your teen will appreciate your support, your respect, and your patience as he or she moves toward victory over obsessions and compulsions, and I wish you both success. Thank you for caring.

Tim Sisemore

# recognizing your stuck thoughts and rituals 1

## for you to know

There are many kinds of obsessions (stuck thoughts) and compulsions (rituals) that can trouble you, and they may change over time. Learning to recognize them can help you overcome them.

In the classroom, Marci seemed to act like everyone else. But in private, she really struggled. Her mind was almost always on trying not to get sick. She worried about being around anyone who had the slightest sniffle, and she waited till she got home to go to the bathroom so she didn't have to use a public one—and so others wouldn't see how long she spent washing her hands after she went. She also feared that something bad might happen to her mom if she didn't tap her foot ten times every time this worry crossed her mind, which was often. Marci held it together fairly well around her friends, but these stuck thoughts and rituals broke loose when she got home.

Marci had only a couple of the common problems that make up obsessive-compulsive disorder. We'll call obsessions "stuck thoughts" as they are worries that are hard to shake (like Marci's worries about getting sick or something happening to her mom). We'll call compulsions "rituals" as they are things you do over and over (like Marci's washing her hands and tapping her foot), usually to try to control stuck thoughts.

Since you're reading this, it's likely you've had some stuck thoughts or rituals. The first step to beating them is to recognize them.

# for you to do

Think through the past couple of days. How many of these stuck thoughts have you had? List the thoughts you come up with.

#_____ _____.

#_____ _____.

#_____ _____.

#_____ _____.

#_____ _____.

Go back through your list and rank them from the most bothersome to the least bothersome, putting a 1 by the most annoying, and so forth.

What are some of the rituals that you experience? Once again, think through the past couple of days and list all the rituals you remember doing.

a. _____

b. _____

c. _____

d. _____

e. _____

Good job!

# wrapping it up

Often certain rituals go with certain stuck thoughts. It doesn't have to be just one. Write the letters (a, b, c, and so on) of the rituals that tend to go with each of your stuck thoughts:

Stuck thought #1 leads to ritual(s): \_\_\_\_\_, \_\_\_\_\_, \_\_\_\_\_, \_\_\_\_\_.

Stuck thought #2 leads to ritual(s): \_\_\_\_\_, \_\_\_\_\_, \_\_\_\_\_, \_\_\_\_\_.

Stuck thought #3 leads to ritual(s): \_\_\_\_\_, \_\_\_\_\_, \_\_\_\_\_, \_\_\_\_\_.

Stuck thought #4 leads to ritual(s): \_\_\_\_\_, \_\_\_\_\_, \_\_\_\_\_, \_\_\_\_\_.

Stuck thought #5 leads to ritual(s): \_\_\_\_\_, \_\_\_\_\_, \_\_\_\_\_, \_\_\_\_\_.

Some stuck thoughts aren't really connected to any rituals. They're just kind of there. List any of your stuck thoughts that don't seem to lead to rituals.

_____

_____

_____

Some rituals just reduce nervousness and aren't related to stuck thoughts. Was this true of any of yours? List any rituals that aren't related to stuck thoughts.

_____

_____

_____

Are your symptoms worse than you thought, not so bad, or about what you figured?

_____

_____

_____

# 2 how do stuck thoughts and rituals affect your life?

## for you to know

As if it isn't bad enough to wrestle with stuck thoughts and rituals, for many teens these symptoms can have a big impact on many areas of their lives—particularly in friendships and self-confidence. In some ways these "side effects" can be worse than the stuck thoughts and rituals themselves.

Jamaal doesn't really appreciate his new nickname, Mr. Perfect. Though he has really tried not to, he still has to keep every paper straight in his organizer and catches himself straightening up his friends' papers. He used to feel good about himself and thought he was pretty popular and cool. But now that his stuck thoughts and rituals have gotten worse, he doesn't go out with friends much because he just doesn't want to hear the teasing. He has to go to school but wouldn't if he didn't have to. Though his friends say they're just teasing, Jamaal doesn't find it very funny. Having OCD is a pain.

# for you to do

Have others—family, friends, or teachers—noticed your rituals? What kinds of things have they said about them?

Have others pointed out that you've changed in some way since OCD became a bigger problem for you? Can you remember what they said?

_____

_____

_____

How do you think your stuck thoughts and rituals have impacted your relationship with your parents? Have your parents been helpful or do they make you feel worse?

_____

_____

_____

How have your stuck thoughts and rituals impacted your relationships with your friends? Have your friends been helpful or do they make you feel worse?

_____

_____

_____

Are there places or activities that make you uncomfortable or that you try to avoid because of these symptoms?

_____

_____

_____

Since stuck thoughts and some rituals are often "invisible," only you know about them. How have these changed the way you feel about yourself?

_____

_____

_____

How do your symptoms affect the sense of control you have over your life?

_____

_____

_____

What is the single biggest change in your life that is due to OCD?

_____

_____

_____

Keep these changes in your life in mind as you work through this book, because knowing how much OCD affects your life can give you motivation to fight it.

# wrapping it up

As you went through the exercise, did you discover some ways OCD has affected your life that you hadn't noticed before? If so, what were they?

_____

_____

_____

Can you think of any other ways that OCD has affected your social life or your self-esteem?

_____

_____

_____

How does what you've learned in this exercise affect your thinking and feeling about OCD?

_____

_____

_____

# 3 imagining yourself free from OCD

## for you to know

Often it's helpful to imagine your destination as you begin a journey. As you begin working on your OCD, imagining life without it can motivate you to keep going.

It wasn't until Carlota talked to her school counselor that she realized how much time her stuck thoughts and rituals were costing her. Now she knew why she felt so stressed and frustrated—her free time was filled with worries and rituals. Tired of all this, Carlota was ready to free up more time to hang out with friends and play video games. She missed those things and planned to work hard on her OCD so she could win back her free time.

Wonder how much time your stuck thoughts and rituals are costing you?

# for you to do

Think first about your rituals, like doing things a certain number of times or checking the doors on your house before leaving for school. About how much time do you think you spend doing these things on a typical day? Run through a whole day in your mind to come up with your guesstimate.

I spend about _____ (hours) and _____ (minutes) a day on my rituals.

What problems do they cause you (for example, having to get up early, take more time doing things, go out of your way to avoid situations, etc.)?

_____

_____

_____

Now think about your stuck thoughts, like worrying that someone you love will get hurt if you don't avoid all the cracks in the pavement on the way to school. Try to estimate how much time you spend with these thoughts on your mind in a given day.

I spend about _____ (hours) and _____ (minutes) a day on my stuck thoughts.

What problems do they cause you (for example, getting distracted at school, changing your routines, causing you to avoid being with friends, etc.)?

_____

_____

_____

Daily time OCD takes from me (ritual time + stuck thought time) =

_____ hours, _____ minutes

Think about this: Each hour per day you spend on OCD means 365 hours a year. That's about the same number of hours that you'd spend if you had to go to school for your entire summer break!

# wrapping it up

How do you feel now that you've figured out how much time your symptoms take from you?

_____

_____

_____

List some things you'll do with the time you have once you overcome OCD—for example, having an extra hour a day for friends or learning to play the guitar or doing homework (well, maybe not).

_____

_____

_____

List three words to describe your thoughts and feelings about getting that much time back.

_____      _____      _____

Take a moment to close your eyes and imagine your new life. How does it feel? How is your social life better? How much freer do you feel without the burden of your stuck thoughts and rituals? How does it feel to imagine waking up in the morning without stuck thoughts and rituals? Don't write anything here ... just enjoy imagining.

Overcoming OCD will make you feel more control over and confidence in your life as you will have beaten a powerful adversary!

## for you to know

OCD symptoms vary from minor bothers to major hassles. You can begin to get better by learning to track how bad the symptoms are and what makes them better or worse.

For years Katie worried about doing something wrong, and more recently she had been almost paralyzed by the urge to pray for forgiveness many times a day. This urge made it hard for her to concentrate in class and even to pay attention when she was watching movies. Katie became so frustrated that she decided to try to figure out when her symptoms got worse. She noticed that she worried the most intensely the day after she stayed up late doing her homework. Realizing this, she was able to predict when her symptoms might be at their worst and to get some control over them. Knowing how to rate how severe her stuck thoughts were helped Katie recognize them better, plan a strategy to fight them, and track the improvement as they became less severe.

# for you to do

Choose one of your stuck thoughts or rituals that bothers you most and think about how much it bothers you based on the following scale:

## OCD Rater

1 = The thought (or impulse to do a ritual) crossed my mind, but I went on doing what I was doing.

2 = I thought about it for a minute, but shook it off and carried on.

3 = It made me nervous, and I felt I needed to do something (like a ritual) to ease my nervousness.

4 = It really bothered me. I couldn't keep my mind on what I was doing and felt very strong urges to do a ritual.

5 = It overwhelmed me. I was lost in worry and/or felt I couldn't help doing the ritual.

Choose a time when you're not incredibly busy and take the time to notice and record each time you catch yourself in the act of a stuck thought or ritual. Fill out the form on the next page until you have caught yourself ten times.

| Time of Day | What I Was Doing | Rating |
|---|---|---|
| | | 1 2 3 4 5 |
| | | 1 2 3 4 5 |
| | | 1 2 3 4 5 |
| | | 1 2 3 4 5 |
| | | 1 2 3 4 5 |
| | | 1 2 3 4 5 |
| | | 1 2 3 4 5 |
| | | 1 2 3 4 5 |
| | | 1 2 3 4 5 |
| | | 1 2 3 4 5 |

# wrapping it up

During what activities or times of day did your OCD seem more severe?

_____

_____

_____

During what activities or times of day did your OCD seem not so bad?

_____

_____

_____

What might explain why your stuck thoughts or rituals are worse at those times? More stress? More free time to think about them? Being around (or away from) certain people or situations?

_____

_____

_____

Did you notice anything about how you reacted differently (had stronger urge for a ritual, felt shaky or nervous, etc.) when the stuck thoughts were stronger compared to when they weren't?

_____

_____

_____

Keep tracking your OCD, even if only in your head, as this will be a useful skill.

# recognizing your triggers     5

| for you to know |
| --- |
| Stuck thoughts and rituals aren't always as random as they may seem. If you look closer, often there are places, times, or activities that stir them up. These are called triggers. |

Enrique felt like his stuck thoughts owned him. They seemed to pop up all of the time, and he thought there was no escaping them. He struggled to control his rituals in public, but doing so wore him out and made him feel worse once he got home. One day, though, his best friend, Michael, asked, "How come you always start worrying about your mom when you're driving? Seems like every time we're in your car you bring it up or want to make sure she's okay."

Michael helped Enrique to see a trigger for OCD: a place, time, or activity that increases the likelihood of worries and rituals. Michael helped his friend feel less trapped by his stuck thoughts. Knowing your triggers can help you feel freer and start to fight feisty thoughts and actions. This activity invites you to learn some of your own triggers.

# for you to do

Think of your top two stuck thoughts and rituals. For twenty-four hours, keep a record of where you are and what's going on when you notice these worries or rituals popping up.

**Stuck thought #1:** _____

| Time | Where I Was | What I Was Doing | Who I Was With |
|------|-------------|------------------|----------------|
|      |             |                  |                |
|      |             |                  |                |
|      |             |                  |                |
|      |             |                  |                |
|      |             |                  |                |
|      |             |                  |                |
|      |             |                  |                |

**Stuck thought #2:** _____

| Time | Where I Was | What I Was Doing | Who I Was With |
|------|-------------|------------------|----------------|
|      |             |                  |                |
|      |             |                  |                |
|      |             |                  |                |
|      |             |                  |                |
|      |             |                  |                |
|      |             |                  |                |
|      |             |                  |                |

**Ritual #1:** _____

| Time | Where I Was | What I Was Doing | Who I Was With |
|------|-------------|------------------|----------------|
|      |             |                  |                |
|      |             |                  |                |
|      |             |                  |                |
|      |             |                  |                |
|      |             |                  |                |
|      |             |                  |                |
|      |             |                  |                |

**Ritual #2:** _____

| Time | Where I Was | What I Was Doing | Who I Was With |
|------|-------------|------------------|----------------|
|      |             |                  |                |
|      |             |                  |                |
|      |             |                  |                |
|      |             |                  |                |
|      |             |                  |                |
|      |             |                  |                |
|      |             |                  |                |

Now take a couple of minutes to think of any other triggers you might have that you didn't experience today but have noticed in the past. Write below any you came up with.

_____

_____

# wrapping it up

Based on this activity, list the most common trigger for each of your top stuck thoughts and rituals. You might come up with more than one.

Stuck thought #1 _____ Trigger _____

Stuck thought #2 _____ Trigger _____

Ritual #1 _____ Trigger _____

Ritual #2 _____ Trigger _____

Think about your triggers for a minute. Can you find any things they have in common (time, people you're with, being tired, etc.)?

_____

_____

Are there any of these triggers you might be able to avoid or prevent?

_____

_____

Are there some of these you simply can't avoid (like homework, bedtime, or watching TV)?

_____

_____

Finally, are there any you could avoid but really shouldn't (like being at the mall with friends) because the activity is too important to avoid?

_____

_____

# ranking your symptoms on the stairs of cares

---

## for you to know

Battling stuck thoughts and rituals can be challenging because you have to face the symptoms head-on. It is generally a good idea to begin with less troubling things to build confidence to take on the tougher ones.

---

Kumiko is a great student and typically manages to solve any problem she faces. But her OCD is a different story. Her approach has been to just tough it out and stop her rituals. Will power hasn't done the trick, and she is disheartened as she repeatedly turns the lights on and off and feels almost helpless to stop.

Kumiko's strategy is pretty common, but it often doesn't work. OCD is stubborn, and you can easily want to give in. The trick may be to start small and work your way up, working on the easier things before tackling the harder ones.

This activity will help you sort out which things are the hardest and which are not as challenging.

# for you to do

OCD has lots of ways to get on your nerves: worrisome thoughts, repeated actions, making you avoid certain places or activities, and so forth. Think about these three categories (stuck thoughts, rituals, things you avoid). List ten of these that bother you and don't worry about putting them in any order just yet.

1. _____    6. _____

2. _____    7. _____

3. _____    8. _____

4. _____    9. _____

5. _____    10. _____

Now think about which might be the easiest to battle and which would be the most difficult. Then rank them from the easiest to hardest, writing one down on each step of the "Stairs of Cares." This will help you choose which problems to work on first. As you "walk" up the stairs, you'll be growing in skills and confidence to be free from OCD.

# wrapping it up

Have you had any experiences like Kumiko's, where you felt you just couldn't change your behavior no matter how hard you tried? Briefly describe them.

_____

_____

_____

_____

How does ranking your cares change the way you think or feel about them?

_____

_____

_____

_____

Look at the bottom step and think about working to overcome it. Write a brief pep talk to get yourself psyched.

_____

_____

_____

_____

# 7 naming your stuck thoughts and rituals

---

## for you to know

Often it's helpful to imagine your destination as you begin a journey. As you begin working on your OCD, imagining life without it can motivate you to keep going.

---

In his quiet moments, Jerry knows that he won't get sick if he uses the school restroom. Nobody else gets sick. Yet when he gets near it, he feels nervous and scared. The idea that germs are waiting for him overcomes him, and he turns away. He immediately feels relief—and frustration that he gave in once again. When his counselor suggested naming his stuck thought "Germ-man," Jerry found power to fight as he challenged the ideas "Germ-man" was putting in his head.

Some stuck thoughts and rituals have a grain of truth (there are germs in the bathroom, for sure); others are pretty unreasonable (turning the light off six times will not keep you from failing a test). To beat them, you have to see them for what they are: your enemies who are trying to deceive you. Giving them a name helps you separate these from the rest of your mind and prepares you to argue with them.

# for you to do

We'll work with your top four troublesome stuck thoughts and/or rituals, encouraging you to think through the reason you do each, giving it a name, and drawing a comic face to represent it. You might look back at the Stairs of Cares in Activity 6 for ideas.

Describe the reason that you do stuck thought, ritual, or pattern #1. For example, "I close the door six times because I think it will keep me from having an accident" could be named "Doora the Explora"; or "I count to twelve in my head to keep me from doing bad things that pop into my head" might be named "the dirty dozen.")

Describe it: _____

_____

Name it: _____

Give it a face:

Describe the reason that you do stuck thought, ritual, or pattern #2.

_____

_____

Name it: _____

Give it a face:

23

Describe the reason that you do stuck thought, ritual, or pattern #3.

_____

_____

Name it: _____

Give it a face:

Describe the reason that you do stuck thought, ritual, or pattern #4.

_____

_____

Name it: _____

Give it a face:

# wrapping it up

On a scale of 1 to 10, with 1 being "No problem" and 10 being "I really believe it deep down," how convincing are each of the stuck thoughts or rituals you named?

Name: _____ Score: _____

Name: _____ Score: _____

Name: _____ Score: _____

Name: _____ Score: _____

Have you ever thought of these stuck thoughts or rituals as outside yourself and not belonging to you?

_____

How does naming them help you separate yourself from them?

_____

_____

How does it feel to think that they are not really part of you but invaders?

_____

_____

How might this view of them change your approach to overcoming them?

_____

_____

# 8 identifying your irrational thoughts

Justin angrily turned after he was bumped while getting a book from his locker. He was just about to say something rude to the boy who bumped him when Rene, who had seen the incident, stopped him. "Justin, ease up. That guy tripped coming down the hall and bumped you accidentally. He didn't mean it."

This story shows that emotion comes from your opinion or thoughts about events, not from the truth of the events themselves. The truth here was that the bump was an accident. Justin, though, assumed someone meant to push him. His anger was the result of misinterpreting what happened. Rene's explanation changed Justin's thinking and thus his feeling. Learning that feelings can come from mistaken beliefs is key to understanding stuck thoughts.

# for you to do

Feelings largely depend on your thinking. The pattern looks like this:

*What Happens → What You Believe About It → Your Emotional Response*

Let's apply this to Justin's situation:

He is bumped → "Somebody is challenging me!" → Anger

But after Rene explains what happened:

He is bumped → "It was an accident." → Calm

See the difference? What you believe affects how you feel. The stuck thoughts of OCD follow the same pattern. For example:

There are some germs on the doorknob → "I know if I touch the doorknob I'll get germs and get really sick." → Anxiety and avoiding the doorknob

The middle part is a big piece of OCD. Most people know there are germs but don't think they'll get sick. Changing that thinking is important to gaining control over OCD.

**Think of three of your stuck thoughts and chart them below:**

Stuck thought: _____

*What Happens*      *→ What You Believe About It*      *→ Your Emotional Response*

_____→ _____→ _____

Stuck thought: _____

*What Happens*      *→ What You Believe About It*      *→ Your Emotional Response*

_____→ _____→ _____

Stuck thought: _____

*What Happens*      *→ What You Believe About It*      *→ Your Emotional Response*

_____→ _____→ _____

# wrapping it up

For each of the three stuck thoughts you just described, briefly explain why it is not logical, or why it is probably inaccurate in reality.

Stuck thought #1

_____

_____

Stuck thought #2

_____

_____

Stuck thought #3

_____

_____

Was this part easy or hard for you? Why do you think so? If it was hard, the next exercise will help.

_____

_____

# exaggeration or distortion? how to tell

## for you to know

OCD lives on irrational thoughts that may trick you into believing them. Knowing how to sort the true worries from the distorted ones will help you gain control over your OCD.

Rosalia was proud that she now had a driver's license and could drive herself to school every day, but she had started worrying a lot about having a wreck. She felt better when she closed the car door four times before starting the engine, believing this would keep her from having a wreck. Still, she wouldn't tell her friends why she was doing this because she knew deep down that it didn't make sense.

# for you to do

People with OCD have two main ways of distorting the way things really are. First, there is worrying about things that pretty much could never happen. For example, you might fear that someone will die if you don't tap the table six times. The feelings in OCD can make this seem like a real danger, but if you get some distance from the feelings, you realize there's no way this is true: it is a distortion.

The second type is trickier, for here you worry about a real danger that is pretty unlikely, but blow it up to be much bigger than it really is. This was where Rosalia started. Sure she might have a wreck, but there is really only a small chance of that. This possibility is probably not worth the amount of worry she's putting into it: it is an exaggeration. Then she combines it with a distortion when she thinks that closing the car door four times keeps her from having a wreck.

List some of your stuck thoughts and note whether they are exaggerations or distortions:

Stuck thought: _____ ☐ Exaggeration ☐ Distortion

Stuck thought: _____ ☐ Exaggeration ☐ Distortion

Stuck thought: _____ ☐ Exaggeration ☐ Distortion

Stuck thought: _____ ☐ Exaggeration ☐ Distortion

Do you have any rituals that are exaggerations or distortions? Washing your hands to get rid of germs would be an exaggeration.

Ritual: _____ ☐ Exaggeration ☐ Distortion

Ritual: _____ ☐ Exaggeration ☐ Distortion

Ritual: _____ ☐ Exaggeration ☐ Distortion

Ritual: _____ ☐ Exaggeration ☐ Distortion

# wrapping it up

Since stuck thoughts and rituals often go together, they can form combos, or combinations, of irrational thoughts. Do you have some combos with a little of both (like Rosalia's exaggeration about the wreck combined with a ritual that is a distortion)? If so, list them below:

## Combos

Stuck Thought: _____ (☐ Exaggeration ☐ Distortion) goes with

Ritual: _____ (☐ Exaggeration ☐ Distortion).

Stuck Thought: _____ (☐ Exaggeration ☐ Distortion) goes with

Ritual: _____ (☐ Exaggeration ☐ Distortion).

It is important to identify both parts and see how they work together. Usually the ritual helps ease the anxiety of the stuck thought, but you need to see the problem with both to fight and overcome them.

# 10 being realistic about distorted and exaggerated thinking

## for you to know

Since feelings can make distorted and exaggerated thinking seem rational, learning how to be more realistic is a step toward mastering your stuck thoughts and rituals.

Will was tough on erasers. He went through one a week. He finally confided in Mary that he secretly believed that his teachers would give him an F on papers unless they were perfectly neat and showed no signs of erasures.

"Will, you don't really believe you'll get an F if your paper isn't neat, do you?" she asked.

"I know it's silly, Mary, but I get really tense worrying about it, and erasing is the only thing that helps," Will replied.

"Think about it, Will. Who do you know that ever got an F just because their paper was not perfectly neat? Come on, you've seen my handwriting. No penmanship awards for me, but my grades are as good as yours."

Mary's words got Will to thinking about what the odds really were that his stuck thought would ever come true.

# for you to do

Most people understand distortions aren't really true (Will knew deep down that he wouldn't get an F for a stray pencil mark here and there). Teens with distortions usually realize they're not logical, but they just *seem* to be real when you're focused on them.

For your distortions, finish the statement below:

"Even though I feel nervous when I think (*write out your distortion*)

_____

I know in my heart that the truth really is that it will never happen."

Try it on one more.

"Even though I feel nervous when I think (*write out your distortion*)

_____

I know in my heart that the truth really is that it will never happen."

Exaggerations are a little more challenging. How likely is it that you will get sick if you touch the doorknob on a public restroom? Sure there are germs, and there is the outside chance you might get sick from them. Think of how many doorknobs you touch in a day; what are the odds of this making you sick—maybe 1 in 1000, or lower? But if you have OCD, you feel like the odds are at least 500 out of 1000. You can recognize distorted thinking by thinking through what the odds *really* are and comparing them to what they *feel* like when you are facing them.

Now pick one of your exaggerations to work on.

When you're fighting this stuck thought or ritual, it *feels* like the odds of the bad thing happening are _____ out of 100.

Think about this more. Consider why other people aren't as troubled by it. Think about past times you've done this and nothing bad happened. Analyze like a computer to consider what the chances *really* are of this happening.

The real odds are something like _____ out of 100.

If you're not sure, talk with a parent or friend to get their estimate.

Now make it into a statement:

"To me, the odds of _____ happening feel like _____ out of

100, but when I really think about it, they're more likely _____ out of 100."

Try this on another exaggeration.

"To me, the odds of _____ happening feel like _____ out of

100, but when I really think about it, they're more likely _____ out of 100."

# wrapping it up

You are now taking the first step to arguing with stuck thoughts and rituals that are, putting it plainly, lies that OCD tells you.

Memorize the statements you completed above. Then take one morning or afternoon and practice saying them to yourself when you face your distortions and exaggerations during that time.

Describe your experience. Was it hard to remember to do? Was it easy or hard to do? Did it change the way you felt? Add any other thoughts you have about the experience.

_____

_____

_____

_____

_____

You're off to a good start. Keep practicing.

# 11 controlling the need for control

## for you to know

Most of the irrational thinking and behavior around OCD involves trying to feel more control over what happens than you really have. But you actually have more power when you gain control over your need for control.

Tony felt better after he called Kyle to make sure he didn't hurt his feelings at school. The problem, though, is that Kyle and all of his friends are tiring of Tony's asking them if he hurt their feelings all the time. Tony's stuck thought is a worry that he'll lose his friends if he says or does something that offends them. His only relief is asking them to make sure, the ritual that eases his worry.

Notice what's happening. Tony is trying to control his friendships by being nice—*too* nice. He then tries to control his nervousness by asking for reassurance. Do you see the real problem? Tony may lose friends by trying so hard to control his relationships.

# for you to do

What do each of your OCD symptoms try to give you control over?

#1 This stuck thought/ritual/pattern (*fill in the blank*) _____

gives me a sense that I can control _____

_____


#2 This stuck thought/ritual/pattern _____

gives me a sense that I can control _____

_____


#3 This stuck thought/ritual/pattern _____

gives me a sense that I can control _____

_____


Now for each, can you think of how they can backfire? How might each cause you to *lose* control over something?

Stuck thought/ritual/pattern #1 _____

_____

Stuck thought/ritual/pattern #2 _____

_____

Stuck thought/ritual/pattern #3 _____

_____

# wrapping it up

You're now catching on to one of the secrets of defeating OCD: seeing how the need to control things can control you in ways you don't want.

For each of the symptoms you used, write a sentence explaining why it doesn't control what it wants you to think it does, and one that states a better way to think about it. (For example, Tony might write, "I can't control how people think about me because I'm not their boss. I can be thoughtful, be kind, and listen to them because these are things good friends do.")

Stuck thought/ritual/pattern #1

_____

_____

_____

Stuck thought/ritual/pattern #2

_____

_____

_____

Stuck thought/ritual/pattern #3

_____

_____

_____

Now you're getting control of OCD instead of it telling you what it wants you to control!

# looking logically at your stuck thoughts 12

## for you to know

Stuck thoughts must be seen for the irrational things they are, no matter how strong your feelings are. Seeing why they aren't logical will empower you to overcome them.

Every day, Robert wrestled with the thought that he might get into trouble at school if he didn't tap the door on his way into every class. Though he knew it probably wasn't true, his powerful anxious feelings convinced him to keep tapping. Robert's counselor understood but explained how anxious feelings are like car alarms, which are designed to go off when someone is breaking into a car, signaling danger. But most of us hear them going off accidentally so often that we almost ignore them. They are still loud, but they don't make us anxious. Stuck thoughts can set off our "nervous alarms," which are quite loud in making us feel there's danger. But, as is usually true when you hear a car alarm, there's no real danger. Stuck thoughts just make you feel like there is.

This explanation sort of clicked for Robert, but he still had a hard time seeing how his stuck thoughts were false; he really felt not tapping would lead to trouble.

# for you to do

It's tough to fight stuck thoughts since they lead to very strong feelings of anxiety. They convince you that there is a serious danger ahead—but they are liars. For a few minutes, try to set aside feelings and look at your stuck thoughts logically. Choose one stuck thought to start with.

My stuck thought tells me that this bad thing will happen: _____

_____

_____

unless I do this: _____

_____

_____ .

Now be the defense attorney and present any evidence for the truth of the stuck thought. (Robert might say, "I've always tapped the door before walking into a classroom and have never gotten into trouble at school, so it must work.")

_____

_____

_____

_____

_____

_____

_____ .

Next, be the prosecutor who has to prove your stuck thought is a lie. Some questions you might ask yourself: Has the dreaded thing happened to other people? If it's so bad, why doesn't anybody else worry like I do? What is the worst that could happen if the bad thing actually did happen? You might also look back at the odds that you figured out in Activity 10. Finally, explain why the defense argument is not logical.

_____

_____

_____

_____

_____

_____

_____

_____

_____

_____

Now repeat the activity with other stuck thoughts.

# wrapping it up

Now you be the judge. The evidence should argue that the stuck thought is guilty of lying to you. Do you agree? If so, which argument was most helpful in convincing you?

_____

_____

You probably suspected all along that the stuck thought wasn't true. Why do you think it is so hard to act on logic instead of feeling?

_____

_____

What might help you to fight the strong feelings that stuck thoughts produce?

_____

_____

Two good ideas for this are to remind yourself of the argument that convinced you and to have others remind you to use your logic.

# getting psyched to fight 13

## for you to know

Battling OCD takes more than just logic; you have to fight feeling with feeling. The anxious feelings of OCD are best overpowered by feelings of determination.

Sonja was encouraged when she convinced herself that her mother would not die if Sonja didn't say the alphabet before leaving the house. But when morning came and she headed for the door, the fear was intense. She shook her head in frustration as she started: A, B, C …

Feelings motivate us more that simple reason does. We've all called a friend to chat when we should have been doing our homework. Talking brings pleasure and tempts us, even though we know we ought to do the homework. If that's true of normal emotions, how much more will it be true of resisting the powerful feelings of OCD?

# for you to do

Let's get you fired up to fight so that you do better than Sonja did. We'll work on three feelings to help you win.

## Anger

How do you feel when someone lies to you? Why?

_____

_____

Think of your OCD as a person who is lying to you and causing all the problems that go with your OCD. What would you say to that person?

_____

_____

Maybe even better, imagine yourself telling this person off for lying to you and tricking you into believing the stuck thought.

## Determination

When sports teams face a challenge, the coach pulls them together and gives them a pep talk to build a focus and commitment to working hard to beat a tough opponent. What might you say to yourself to motivate yourself to battle the lies of stuck thoughts?

_____

_____

## Hope

Imagining victory aids in winning. Describe the feeling you'll have when you beat your lying stuck thought.

_____

_____

# wrapping it up

Let's pull these approaches together to maximize motivation. If you are more of a visual person, draw a picture in the space below that represents your determination to defeat the thoughts and false alarms of OCD. If you are more of a word person, write a brief pep talk to yourself. It will be a challenge, but you're going to win. Believe that, not your OCD.

# 14 stop that thought!

## for you to know

One of the tricky things about stuck thoughts is that they are so frequent that they feel automatic. A big step in beating OCD is learning to catch and interrupt your obsessive thinking.

Can you remember a scene like this from a movie? One of the characters is upset or panicked and is yelling or fussing or just plain freaking out. A calmer character approaches and slaps or shakes the panicked person, breaking up the episode.

Stuck thoughts are much like that: They can come over you and control you— sometimes without your being aware of them. They may keep rolling along unless you startle yourself out of the pattern.

# for you to do

Thought-stopping is a skill that is pretty simple: once you catch yourself obsessing, you jolt yourself out of it. There are two parts to it.

First, as soon as you notice the stuck thought, yell "Stop!" Since that might look a bit weird in public, you might just yell it in your head when you're not alone.

Second, like the slap in the movie scenes, a mild pain can sometimes help. A couple of suggestions are wearing a rubber band around your wrist and snapping it as you say stop, or pinching yourself gently as you say it. You might think of something else. Write your choice below:

_____

Now practice. For the next twenty-four hours, really focus on catching yourself obsessing and interrupt yourself with a firm "Stop!" and mild pain. As you get better at this, you may drop the pain part. This won't stop the stuck thoughts (though it may help), but it breaks them up so you're in a better position to fight them.

# wrapping it up

Briefly describe your thought-stopping experience after doing it for a day. Any surprises? Frustrations? How consistently did you use it?

_____

_____

_____

_____

As you did this, what effect did it have on your obsessing? Did it help, hurt, or change your patterns in any way?

_____

_____

_____

_____

If you had trouble being consistent, think of a way to improve and note it below.

_____

_____

Remember: this isn't supposed to stop stuck thoughts, just disrupt them.

# arguing with your stuck thoughts 15

---

## for you to know

Once you catch yourself obsessing, you can argue with your stuck thoughts. This will reduce the anxious feelings and make it easier to avoid rituals.

---

Mi Sun stayed up very late every night studying because she feared she would be a failure if she did not do her absolute best in school. She would close her books and turn out the lights only when her mother threatened to ground her if she did not go to bed.

Tired of getting into an argument with her mother every night, Mi Sun began arguing with her stuck thought about perfection. "Nobody is perfect, and I'll still make good grades if I study a little less. Besides, staying up late leaves me sleepy in school so it really hurts my performance. It is a lie that I have to be perfect to be okay. In fact, I'm a better person when I have control over this stuck thought than when I give in to it."

Mi Sun did better when she stopped listening to her stuck thoughts and talked back to them instead.

# for you to do

Imagine yourself having your worst stuck thought right now. Write down what you can say to it to tell it who's boss and why. Call it by a name so you are clear that it doesn't speak for the real you. Try to list at least three reasons why it is not logical.

_____

_____

_____

_____

Now do the same for your second most bothersome stuck thought.

_____

_____

_____

_____

Now try it with one more.

_____

_____

_____

_____

You've got the hang of it. Once you notice that you're having the stuck thought, argue with it. You might write all your arguing points on an index card and keep it with you so you can refer to them if you need to.

# wrapping it up

On a scale of 1 to 10, with 1 being "I couldn't do it at all" and 10 being "I argued down those stuck thoughts every time," how would you rank your success? _____

Now think of how you could move your score up a notch or two (and you don't have to reach 10 to be doing well!).

How could you better remember to argue when you catch yourself obsessing?

_____

_____

Can you think of other arguments to use with your stuck thoughts?

_____

_____

How could you improve your motivation to fight these thoughts, given the strong feelings they produce?

_____

_____

Keep practicing. This is a skill that requires a little work.

# 16 replace that thought!

---

## for you to know

Now that you know how to disrupt obsessive thoughts and to defeat them in debate, you can take the next step by replacing them with pleasant ones.

---

Owen dreaded eating. He was mortally afraid that anything he ate could cause him to get sick to his stomach and throw up. This fear was even worse at school because he worried he might not make it to a bathroom in time. When he was worrying about this he knew that it didn't really make sense, but the thoughts just kept coming.

He noticed one day that once he started talking to his friends while he ate his lunch, the worries eased up. He realized that if he could get his mind on something else, he didn't obsess as badly.

# for you to do

Try a little experiment. Count to twenty in your head but as you do, do *not* think about purple elephants.

Tough, huh? It's the same if you try not to think about your stuck thought. Seems the more you try not to, the more you do it.

Once you stop your obsessive thought, the idea is to get your mind on something else that is comforting, not anxiety inducing. This can be thinking about a favorite person, a happy movie, or an upcoming event you are looking forward to. Maybe the best one is to think of a favorite (preferably upbeat) song that you can sing (if only in your head).

Think about the options and choose the specific thought you want to use when you stop a stuck thought:

_____

For the next twenty-four hours, when you notice you are having a stuck thought, focus your thinking on your replacement thought instead. Good luck!

# wrapping it up

On a scale of 1 to 10 with 1 being "no help at all" and 10 being "worked like a charm," rate how well replacing your thoughts worked in freeing your mind from your stuck thoughts: _____

Most likely your score was somewhere in the middle. Think more closely about your experience. Describe what happened when you tried to replace your stuck thought.

_____

_____

_____

_____

Did you come up with any strategies that helped you do better as the day progressed?

_____ If so, describe the strategy.

_____

_____

For most people, it takes some practice and persistence, with the stuck thought gradually fading into the background as they think the pleasant thought more clearly. Keep working and you'll get it!

## for you to know

Stuck thoughts seem to come when you least want them. One way to get more control over them is to think them on purpose—until you wear them out!

Katerina settled down to watch a few minutes of TV before going to bed, but then there they were again: those unwelcome thoughts that she might get sick and end up vomiting. As usual, she got so upset by these thoughts that she really did start to feel sick to her stomach. Frustrated and tired of losing sleep so many nights, she finally shared her misery with her mom.

"Katerina, those thoughts seem to own you. Why don't you do something to fight back? Have you tried thinking them on purpose till you're sick of the thoughts instead of sick to your stomach?"

So to her room Katerina went and tried to think of nothing *but* getting sick to her stomach. Taking charge felt good, and after a while she felt relaxed enough to drift off to sleep.

# for you to do

Take a lesson from Katerina and try this on one of your stuck thoughts. There are a couple of ways to do this, so choose the one that suits you best.

Make a list of some of the common thoughts that go with the stuck thought you're going to work on. (Katerina might have listed "What if I lose my lunch?" and "Wonder if my dinner will make me sick?")

List of things I think when my thought gets stuck:

_____

_____

_____

_____

_____

_____

If you have a cell phone with a voice recorder, or some other type of audio recorder, try this: Think the thoughts on your list out loud for about ten minutes straight, taping yourself as you do so. Then, when the stuck thought sneaks up on you, take control and just play the tape of your worrying out loud. Play it several times till you get tired of listening to yourself worry. You're getting control of your stuck thought!

The second way to do this is similar but without the tape. Keep your list of common thoughts handy, and when the stuck thought comes, stop what you're doing, pull out the list, and think or talk through it over and over till you get tired of it. Try not to let your mind wander off the stuck thought; you want to be in control of it.

# wrapping it up

After you've done this a few times, write how it felt to think these thoughts on purpose rather than let them sneak up on you:

_____

_____

_____

_____

You may want to take this type of control one step further. Set up one or two times a day when you schedule stuck-thought time. At those times, play your tape or go through your list. When the stuck thoughts come at other times, talk back to them by telling them to wait their turn at the next scheduled worry time.

# 18 don't be fooled by feelings

## for you to know

Even though you're learning to fight stuck thoughts, you may still find that the nervous feelings that go with them are strong. Understanding why will make it easier to cope with them.

Nancy felt her chest tightening as she neared the cafeteria. Her heart beat faster, and she started to tremble. Would today be the day she'd say something stupid while eating with her friends, destroying the popularity she'd worked hard to gain? She marched down the hall with determination, only to slow and stop outside the door. "I couldn't eat anyway, and my friends will think something's wrong if they see how nervous I am," she thought. Nancy turned away and strolled down the hall to the vending machine, feeling better with each step. Maybe she would have only a bag of chips, but it was worth it to avoid the fear and, possibly, shame that awaited her. Yet as she ate her chips, she felt depressed by another defeat. She knew she should have gone to lunch, but her feelings scared her too much.

# for you to do

Ever felt like Nancy? The physical sensations and feelings that come with stuck thoughts can overwhelm you. Even though Nancy knew deep down her fear was irrational, the feelings scared her enough to stop her.

List some of the physical sensations you experience when you have stuck thoughts or rituals. (You might want to wait till you have a battle with them so you can pay close attention to your physical sensations.)

_____

_____

_____

What do you understand about *why* you might have these feelings?

_____

_____

_____

Nancy's feelings are all part of the fight-or-flight response designed to help us either battle a fearsome enemy or get away from it. To fight or run, we need a faster heart rate, heavier breathing, and such. The shaking that Nancy experienced may come from her body being activated and ready to fight or flee. All these reactions prepare us for a danger we face or warn us when we're approaching a place where we've been scared before.

Think about your symptoms. What "danger" are they preparing you for?

_____

_____

Knowing why you have these feelings can help you understand that you need not be afraid of the feelings themselves.

59

# wrapping it up

Let's revisit Nancy for just a minute. Knowing about the fight-or-flight response, which do you think Nancy did? _____

Why do you think she felt better as she walked away from the cafeteria?

_____

_____

_____

Now to the feelings you have when your stuck thoughts strike: do you think the danger you envision is real or exaggerated? _____

Note that the danger doesn't have to be a real one to stir up these feelings. (Think of how nervous you can feel in a scary movie when you know deep down that you're safe.)

What do you do to try to ease the feelings?

_____

_____

_____

How does that help or hurt your stuck thoughts?

_____

_____

_____

# conquering your nervous feelings 19

## for you to know

Understanding the feelings of the fight-or-flight response readies you to fight instead of flee. Using your thinking skills, you can retrain your feelings so they don't sound the "false alarms" caused by stuck thoughts.

Nancy (whom we met in Activity 18) had had enough. She was ready to fight the feelings that kept her from going to the cafeteria at school to eat with her friends. She armed herself with her best argument against the stuck thought that she would say something to embarrass herself and lose her friends: "We all act silly together, and that's part of the fun. Even if I do say or do something embarrassing, they're my friends and will laugh with me, not at me. These nervous feelings are false alarms because the truth is there's nothing to be scared of."

As Nancy expected, her heartbeat quickened as she neared the cafeteria. She knew now what was going on: the fight-or-flight response. This time, she was determined to fight. She took a deep breath and kept walking, reminding herself that her feelings were a false alarm. She wouldn't lose out on another fun lunch with her friends.

Nancy got her tray, sat next to her friends, and again reminded herself that the nervous feelings wanted her to flee a nonexistent danger. She started talking to her friends and felt her tensions ease. She enjoyed the food and friendship at lunch—but not as much as the thrill of fighting fear and winning!

# for you to do

Look at Nancy's story. See if you can come up with five strategies she used to fight her feelings instead of fleeing because of them.

1. _____

2. _____

3. _____

4. _____

5. _____

Good job. Now use these strategies to make your own plan for your nervous feelings.

_____

_____

_____

_____

_____

_____

_____

Next, try your plan. It may take some practice, but don't let false-alarm feelings stop you from doing what you want or need to do.

# wrapping it up

Nancy likely will have to go through her plan a few more days before going to lunch gets fairly easy. After you've tried your plan about five times, answer these questions.

What's been the hardest part of using your plan?

_____

_____

What adjustments could you make that might help you? (Look back at Nancy's story if you need some help.)

_____

_____

Do your feelings seem to be worse, about the same, or better? Why do you think that is?

_____

_____

Before Nancy conquered her nervous feelings, she found relief by walking away. It is important to realize this action actually *increases* the chances of your having the nervous feelings next time you're in that situation. It's like your body says, "Oh, so there *was* a danger, and I'm glad we got away. We'll stay away from that from now on."

Remember this when you're tempted to flee rather than fight your feelings.

# 20 recognizing your thought loops

## for you to know

Understanding how stuck thoughts and rituals make a loop in your mind can equip you to take a stronger stand against them.

Gavin sighed with relief as he finished tapping the table. Even if only for a few minutes, the relief the magical taps brought him was immense.

Gavin lived in fear that he would suddenly shout out a curse word, something he didn't think was right. The thought came to his mind very often, but especially when he was in public places, like school and the music store he worked in. When the fear welled up in him, only tapping a surface ten times helped. But the problem was that the thought would be back shortly. The relief was only temporary, and he was having to do this more and more. His friends were starting to ask why he tapped things so much. Gavin longed for something that would make his stuck thought go away for good, not just for a minute.

# for you to do

Gavin's story shows how stuck thoughts and rituals often form a loop that might look like this:

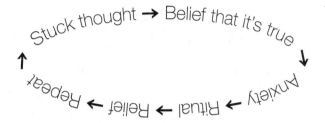

For Gavin, the loop would look like this:

"I might yell a curse word." → "I really might!" → "I feel really nervous."

"Here it comes again!" ← "Whew!" ← "Tap a surface ten times."

65

Now it's your turn. Choose one of your stuck thought/ritual patterns and put it in the loop.

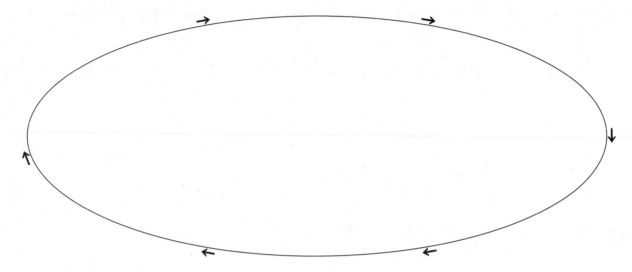

Try one more.

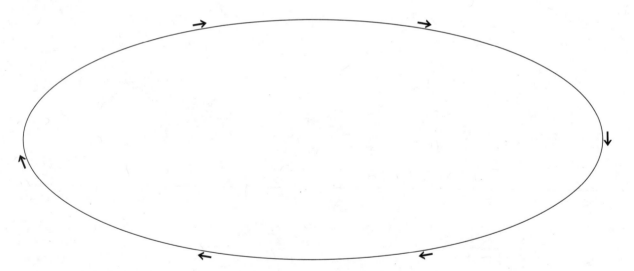

Sometimes the ritual will be more logically related to the stuck thought. For example, washing your hands does indeed get rid of some germs for those who have stuck thoughts about that. That still leads to the thought loop you're learning about.

# wrapping it up

Here's the mystery: if the ritual makes you feel better for a minute, why doesn't it last? Do you have a guess?

_____

_____

Try resisting the ritual a little more than usual for a few hours. What happens when you do so?

_____

_____

Why do you think that happened?

_____

_____

Notice some of the weapons you're gaining in your fight against OCD:

- The "believe it's true" step is attacked by skills in challenging thinking.

- The "anxiety" step is attacked by skills in understanding feelings.

- The "ritual" step is challenged by preventing the ritual and exposing yourself to the things you fear, skills you'll be learning soon.

# 21 how rituals make stuck thoughts worse

## for you to know

Rituals trick you into believing they help when they really don't. Knowing this will give you power to fight them.

Kayla's stuck thought was worrying that she would forget things: her friends' names, phone numbers, and things she was supposed to do. She coped with this worry by constantly writing things down—even things she knew she really didn't have to remember, like the license numbers of her friends' cars and such. She knew it was out of hand, but she still couldn't go anywhere without her sacred scratch pad and pen.

Kayla talked this over with her boyfriend one day, and he questioned why she wrote stuff down when she knew she didn't need it. This got her to thinking, and she realized it made her feel safe from her fear. But if her fear wasn't real, what was she doing? Kayla thought, "It's like being afraid of a lion in the city. You know there isn't one, but you stay in the house to be safe anyway. That just doesn't make sense."

Kayla discovered just one of the reasons why giving in to rituals worsens stuck thoughts. They make you feel safe, but you were safe to start with. Let's learn a few more.

# for you to do

The problem with stuck thoughts is they are never satisfied. Every time you give in to one by performing a ritual, you actually make the stuck thought and the ritual *stronger*! There are several reasons for this. Choose one of your patterns to think about as we look at these.

First, as Kayla realized, the stuck thought gets worse because you think it's real and manage to avoid the danger—but the danger is only in your head. In doing so, you "prove" to yourself the danger was real. After all, why would you do it if you didn't *need* to? Rituals convince you that false fears are true.

Write out how this would apply to your pattern:

_____

_____

_____

Second, rituals also make stuck thoughts worse by giving you a false sense of control over them. Since you can't do anything to truly reduce the fear (since there's no danger anyway), your mind invents an activity that gives you the illusion you're doing something to help. Again, OCD proves to be tricky.

How does your ritual give you a sense of control over your stuck thought?

_____

_____

_____

Finally, rituals make stuck thoughts worse because they treat the "symptom," not the "disease." That is, they act as if the worry is real and temporarily fix it rather than attacking the real problem: the irrational thought.

Describe how your ritual treats the worry as if it were true.

_____

_____

_____

What is the irrational thought that really needs to be treated?

_____

_____

# wrapping it up

One final thing to note is that using rituals to ease the nervousness of stuck thoughts also leads to doing the rituals more.

Think of it this way. If you're feeling thirsty, what do you want to do? _____.

And doing that makes you feel _____.

Anything we do that makes us feel better is a reward. So what will you want to do *next* time you're thirsty? _____.

Yep, the same thing.

So if writing things down makes Kayla feel better when she's nervous, guess what she'll want to do next time? _____

(That was too easy, huh?)

Share your reaction to learning how tricky the relationship between stuck thoughts and rituals is.

_____

_____

# 22 standing your ground against rituals

## for you to know

Rituals are a form of fleeing a false fear; to beat them you must stand and fight for the truth!

Rhiannon knew she was way too scared of getting sick. She thought about it almost constantly, but her nervousness really skyrocketed when she heard a cough, sneeze, or sniffle. This reaction became so bad that she tried to leave the room when she witnessed any of these. It was the only thing that eased her anxiety. But she couldn't leave the house when her sister coughed, nor could she leave the classroom if a schoolmate had a sniffle. Rhiannon then developed the ritual of rubbing her hands on her pant legs five times as if to clean away the germs. She knew this didn't really keep away germs, but it *did* ease her stress. It was beginning to take up so much time that she wasn't getting her work done in class. Something had to give.

Rhiannon told herself that the rubbing was silly and tried not to do it, but she would become more nervous and then give in to the ritual. She was feeling desperate and wanted help.

# for you to do

While Rhiannon was on the right track, she wasn't having success. Let's think about why. First, the story tells us two things she did to reduce her stuck thought about getting sick. They are:

1. _____

2. _____

These illustrate the two main ways to cope with stuck thoughts: avoiding the feared thing or situation (or doing something to comfort your mind, like washing your hands or checking to see if you turned off a light), and finding a "magical" ritual to reduce the fear. Sometimes the rituals simply reduce a vague feeling of stress without a stuck thought.

Choose one of your rituals to work on. What is it?

_____

Describe the feeling or stuck thought that the ritual relieves.

_____

_____

Rituals hang around only because they make you feel better, *not* because they actually solve a problem or prevent the worry. They're actually a way our bodies fool us. There are two solutions. First, you need to stand your ground and not perform the ritual.

How could Rhiannon do this?

_____

_____

How could you do it for your ritual?

_____

_____

This solution is called response prevention: not doing the thing that magically eases your anxiety.

The second is to deliberately face the thing you're afraid of but know you shouldn't be. Rhiannon had to do that when she couldn't leave the classroom, and she needed to do it all the time.

What do you need to do to face the false fear that leads you to avoid some things?

_____

_____

# wrapping it up

Knowing what to do is easier than doing it. Why do you think it is so hard to simply not do the ritual?

_____

_____

_____

Why is it hard to face the false fear your stuck thought causes you?

_____

_____

_____

# 23 hanging in there with nervous feelings

## for you to know

Rituals shortcut the process of overcoming anxiety by keeping you from sticking it out. If you hang in there when dealing with false fear, it will go away after a while.

After the movie, Brad winced as he walked out of the dark theater into the sunlight. It never occurred to him to duck back into the building because he knew in a few seconds his eyes would adjust to the brightness. As he thought about this, it hit him. If he hung tough with his anxieties instead of doing his rituals, would his body adjust? It was worth a try.

Brad had stumbled onto a great idea. If he kept going back into the dark, his eyes would never get to adjust. Doing rituals to ease the anxiety of OCD is the same thing. You have to stay with the feelings for a while, and the anxiety will go away.

# for you to do

To begin, let's learn to rank the nervousness you feel when tempted to do rituals. Remember, sometimes it will be because of stuck thoughts, sometimes not. Let's use a 1 to 10 scale.

Use these guidelines:

1 = don't even notice the feelings

2 = feel just a touch nervous

3 = feel uneasy, but can cope

4 = thinking about my ritual to get some relief

5 = pretty uncomfortable, wanting to do my ritual

6 = nervous, wanting badly to do something to help

7 = so nervous I feel my heart beating faster or my breath getting heavy

8 = so nervous that I'm almost shaky

9 = can't take it; have to do my ritual or something

10 = feel like I'm having a panic attack

Next time you have your stuck thought or feel tempted to do your ritual, see how far up the scale you can go before you give in. Don't worry about what your rating is at this point. Just practice monitoring your feelings and noting how intense they are before you give in.

Do ten scores for the next ten times you feel like doing your ritual. List them below:

_____  _____  _____  _____  _____

_____  _____  _____  _____  _____

What was the lowest score at which you did your ritual? _____

What was the highest score you got to before doing your ritual? _____

# wrapping it up

You'll be learning more skills to help you hang in there, but try a couple of times to see if you can beat your highest score before doing your ritual.

What was it like staying with the feeling instead of doing the ritual?

_____

_____

Did you come up with any strategies on your own to help you stay with it?

_____

_____

Another way to practice this is to track how long you can go from the first thought of the ritual until you do it. Use your watch and time yourself five times:

_____ seconds _____ seconds _____ seconds _____ seconds _____ seconds

Did it get easier or harder as you went along? _____

# 24 easing your anxiety with deep breaths

## for you to know

Facing your feelings without giving in to your ritual sometimes takes more that arguing with stuck thoughts. You might have to remind your body to relax since the danger isn't real.

Hailey was feeling it. She wanted so badly to turn the car radio on and off, but she knew that had nothing to do with her mom being safe. She was battling the irrational stuck thought that something bad would happen to her mom.

"That's silly. Mom can take care of herself, and there's nothing miraculous about me messing with the radio!" she reminded herself.

But the nervous feelings kept coming. She could feel her heart beat and she felt warm. Hailey told herself there was nothing to fear, but her body was acting as though she were in danger. Her mind knew it was a false alarm, but she needed to settle down her body.

# for you to do

When you have nervous and stuck thoughts, your body responds to them as though the danger were real, preparing you to fight or flee. Your body may hang on to nervous feelings, especially if it is trained to find relief through rituals.

One of the things you can do to take charge of your body is to take deep breaths that tell your body everything is okay, helping it to relax. Here's how. Read this once to get the idea, then try it a couple of times.

> *Sit comfortably in a chair, without slouching. Rest your arms on the armrests or on your legs. Put your feet flat on the floor. Pay attention to the slight pressure you feel from the weight of your body on the chair. Now, take in a deep breath and hold it for five seconds. Then, let it out very slowly, taking as long as you can until you almost need to cough out the last little bit of air. Repeat this, but now pay attention to your body more than to the breath. As you release the breath, notice the sensation of your body sinking into the chair and losing tension. You are telling your body to relax because everything really is okay. On the third breath, you might repeat a statement that denies the stuck thought, like "Relax; my mom is fine, and I don't need to do any rituals."*

Practice this a few times right now. Then try it a few times when you are feeling nervous and fighting off your rituals.

# wrapping it up

Describe the feeling you had after practicing deep breaths a few times when you weren't nervous.

_____

_____

_____

Describe the feeling you had when using deep breaths to battle your nervousness around stuck thoughts and rituals.

_____

_____

_____

On a scale of 1 to 10, when fighting your feelings, how strong were they before the deep breaths? _____

What score would you give your feelings after the deep breaths? _____

Keep practicing your breathing along with the strategies for battling stuck thoughts.

# should others help you 25
## fight your rituals?

## for you to know

Sometimes rituals are like bad habits: you do them without thinking. Having a parent or friend remind you can help you to use your skills.

Karim was always near some hand sanitizer. He reached for it every time he thought he might have touched something that was germy. He knew this wasn't necessary and he wanted to try to resist. The problem was that his ritual was so automatic that he didn't even notice he was doing it many times. Karim knew he couldn't beat his ritual if he wasn't more consistent in fighting it.

Karim's mom had been pretty cool about his OCD. She wanted him to overcome it, but she didn't nag him about it all the time. He turned to her for help. "Mom, I keep using the sanitizer without even knowing when I do it. It's like I'm on autopilot. Could you just say something simple when you see me reaching for it, like 'Karim, what's your plan?' That'll remind me to try to resist it."

She agreed, and it really helped … even though it sometimes aggravated him.

# for you to do

Ever have a hard time catching your rituals like Karim did? You can use most of the skills you're learning on your own, but sometimes catching yourself when you get stuck or are performing a ritual can be difficult. Still, you might feel like going it alone.

List a few reasons you would rather do this on your own.

1. _____

2. _____

3. _____

4. _____

List a few reasons you could use someone reminding you when you are doing rituals or getting stuck.

1. _____

2. _____

3. _____

4. _____

Think it through for a bit. What seems better for you: fighting OCD solo or using a helper? Why do you think so?

_____

# wrapping it up

If you decided to go solo, write down a few ideas on how you can try to catch yourself before you do your rituals.

_____

_____

_____

_____

If you decided you could use some help, list a few qualities of the kind of person who might help.

_____

_____

_____

_____

Based on your list, who will you ask? It can be most anyone that you are around often.

_____

And one bonus if you use a helper: knowing someone else is keeping an eye on you will strengthen you even more to win the battle against OCD.

# 26 disrupting your rituals

## for you to know

Learning to control your rituals just a bit before you try to knock them out altogether can help you feel power over them.

Karim, our friend from Activity 25, was feeling a little better now that he was catching himself when he reached for the hand sanitizer, but the thought of *not* using it made him really nervous. He understood that it was a false fear and that he wouldn't really get sick, but he knew the tension would disappear if he just gave in.

He wondered, "How can I at least make a little progress so I feel I have some control over them? It feels so much like they rule me, and that's not good."

Suddenly, Karim remembered something his basketball coach had said: "If the other team gets in a rhythm and is starting to win, call a time-out to disrupt their flow."

"That might work with my ritual!" he thought. Karim decided he would wait thirty seconds before he used the sanitizer. Even if he did do it, at least it was now a bit more on his terms.

# for you to do

Karim was on to something, for it is often possible to shake up your rituals so they are less automatic and more under your control. There are several ways to do that. Before we look at them, think of one of your rituals to practice with. Write it here:

_____

_____

_____

Be aware that some of these disruptions will work better for your ritual than others, since rituals differ.

**1. Delay the ritual.** This is what Karim did. How could you do that for yours?

_____

_____

**2. Make the ritual less convenient.** In Karim's case, he could put all the hand sanitizer in the upstairs bathroom so he had to go upstairs to use it. How could you make your ritual less convenient?

_____

_____

**3. Change the ritual.** Karim could get rid of the hand sanitizer and use only soap that is in the bathroom. How could you change yours?

_____

_____

**4. Slow the ritual.** Even if Karim decided to rub his hands very slowly with the hand sanitizer, it would change the rhythm of the ritual. How could you do something to slow yours down (for example, count more slowly)?

_____

_____

**5. Shorten the ritual.** Karim could decide to use just a drop of sanitizer and rub his hands back and forth only once. What would a shorter ritual look like for you?

_____

_____

# wrapping it up

Which of these five disruptions seems like something you could do?

_____

_____

Try it for a day, then describe your experience:

_____

_____

Did you feel you gained some control, or did you feel frustrated because it didn't work too well?

_____

_____

If it's working, keep it up. If not, don't lose heart. Try again with another disruption.

If one of these worked, share what it feels like to have some power over your ritual:

_____

_____

# 27 making your rituals impossible

## for you to know

Since you can't do two things at once, some rituals can be overcome simply by planning to do something that makes them impossible to do.

Aisha was getting embarrassed because now you could see thin places in her hair from where she had pulled out hairs. She knew this was a harmful ritual, but it seemed to reduce her feelings of stress. When Aisha kept track of her habit, she found she did it mostly when she watched TV or when she was going to sleep at night.

"If only I could keep my hands from being free to reach for my hair. It's almost automatic, and if they weren't available, I'd be able to stop this before I have to think about wearing a wig to the prom," she thought.

Aisha first tried sitting on her hands when she watched television, and that helped. But her hands still slipped out and found her hair. Her dad suggested that she try to keep her hands busy. She bought some soft modeling clay and kept it by her seat in the den. She made it a plan to work the clay in her hands when watching television. This not only kept her from pulling out her hair but relieved her stress as well.

Bedtimes were more of a challenge. Aisha couldn't busy her hands and try to sleep at the same time. But as her habit got better during the day with the clay, she found she could do better at night by keeping her hands under her pillow. She was pumped because she now felt she could go to the prom without being embarrassed.

# for you to do

Many rituals can be helped by planning to keep busy doing something that makes them impossible. Aisha came up with some good plans. Backup plans for bedtime could have included other things, like putting her hair in a shower cap at night or wearing mittens on her hand so she couldn't grab the hairs. It may take a little creativity, but it can be done.

Let's start by working on a ritual that is a behavior you struggle with. Write it here:

_____

Do you need to find something to busy your whole body (for example, moving to a different part of the house or taking a walk) or just a part (like your hands)?

_____

If a part, which part? _____

Think of three things you could do to keep your body/part occupied so you can't do the ritual (for example, if your ritual is touching doorknobs, you could keep your hands in your pockets when you walk near doorknobs).

1. _____

2. _____

3. _____

Some rituals are in your head, not actions you perform. These include things like counting, praying, and repeating certain phrases. Here you may want to plan to think a pleasant thought that will occupy your mind instead.

What is a mental ritual you'd like to fight? _____

List three things you could plan to think about when tempted by your ritual:

1. _____

2. _____

3. _____

Now you've got a plan. Pick one of your high-risk times for rituals. Start with one contradictory behavior or thought and try it for a few days. If it doesn't do the trick, try another.

# wrapping it up

Briefly describe your experience with making your ritual impossible.

_____

_____

_____

Did you have to try more than one strategy? _____ If so, why do you think
the first one didn't work?

_____

_____

Did *any* of them work? Why or why not?

_____

_____

(If they didn't, hang in there, and try some of the other skills that are still to come.)

Overall, how much did you improve over a week doing this? Did you reduce your
rituals by a third? Cut them in half? What fraction of improvement do you estimate?

_____

# 28 planning to prevent your rituals

## for you to know

Standing up against your rituals is the key to getting rid of them. Since this is a challenge, having a plan is a good idea.

April's belief in God was a big part of her life. She had been raised in a religious family and loved going to services. Since she developed OCD, however, she doubted her faith. She worried often that she might not truly believe in God. Learning that this was a common stuck thought didn't help. All she could do to ease her anxiety was to say a prayer for faith. She knew this was a ritual and not really necessary, but it was hard to stop. Since she always closed her eyes when she prayed, her parents and friends noticed her doing this. April was ready to stop this repetitive prayer and get back to a healthier faith in God.

April met with the counselor at her school to ask for help. The counselor explained to April that she needed to resist the temptation to pray when she knew it was a ritual and not something she really needed to pray about. He helped April make a plan on how to dispute the thoughts and deal with the anxiety she felt. April was excited to have a plan for victory at last!

# for you to do

Like on a dance or sports team, it is crucial to have your players in place before you begin. Here are some things you'll want to cover before you seriously try to avoid your rituals. Let's look at how April might answer them before you try it yourself.

When do I tend to do it most? *"When I'm tired or don't have much to do."*

What is the stuck thought that leads to my ritual? *"Being afraid that I don't really believe in God."*

How do I know the ritual really doesn't work? *"It makes me feel better, but it's a trick. Why would I pray for faith if I didn't believe in God in the first place?"*

How do I know the stuck thought isn't true? *"It's silly, because God is very important to me. It's just my OCD trying to make me miserable."*

What will I say to myself when I start thinking my stuck thought? *"Leave me alone, Doubter. You're a liar, and I know it!"*

What will happen if I resist doing my ritual? *"I'll feel more nervous for a while because it's such a habit."*

What will I do when I feel the stress of resisting the ritual? *"I'll use my deep-breathing skills to tell my body it's a false alarm. I will try to get my mind on something else and remind myself the feelings will pass if I'm patient."*

How will I celebrate when I succeed? *"Every time I win over the ritual, I'll let myself stay on the computer five extra minutes that night."*

Now take one of your rituals and put your plan together.

When do I tend to do it most? _____

What is the stuck thought (if any) that leads to my ritual?

_____

How do I know the ritual really doesn't work?

_____

How do I know the stuck thought isn't true?

_____

What will I say to myself when I start thinking my stuck thought?

_____

What will happen if I resist doing my ritual?

_____

What will I do when I feel the stress of resisting the ritual?

_____

How will I celebrate when I succeed?

_____

# wrapping it up

Take a minute to think if there are any other things you need to prepare for before you resist your rituals. Write down any you come up with.

_____

_____

_____

Draw a picture below that represents your readiness to resist your rituals.

# 29 don't do it!

## for you to know

The way to rid yourself of rituals is to "Just Say No!" A good plan prepares you to do just that. The final step is to turn the plan into action.

April (from Activity 28) had worked hard to give herself the best chance of overcoming her ritual of praying for faith when she was nervous that she didn't believe in God. She set a day to start when she wasn't too busy and figured she wouldn't be tired. She wanted to give this her best shot.

When the day came, April changed her prayer to say, "God, help me beat my OCD." It was tough going, and she didn't win every round. By the end of the day, she figured she'd resisted the ritual about half the time. When she found herself getting discouraged, April remembered the words of her counselor: "Progress, not perfection." She *had* made progress and could choose to feel good about that rather than getting down because she wasn't yet perfect. She would keep trying tomorrow.

# for you to do

Let's follow April's lead. When do you think a good time would be for you to begin your fight with your rituals? Be specific and consider things like being rested and not distracted by busyness.

_____

Fight your rituals for one day, then complete the report below. (You might want to make copies of this so you can use it over and over.)

Day and date: _____ Ritual I fought: _____

I feel I did (*circle one*):     great     well     average     poorly     badly

My guess would be that I resisted my rituals completely about _____ percent of the time today.

I at least put up a fight about _____ percent of the time today.

Things I can do differently tomorrow to help me improve my ratings:

_____

_____

Keep working at it. Rituals don't develop in a day, and beating them can take a little while, too.

# wrapping it up

Write a journal entry for your experience on the first day of resisting rituals, sharing your thoughts, feelings, successes, failures, and attitude about continuing to work at this.

_____

_____

_____

_____

_____

_____

_____

_____

_____

_____

If you're having a hard time, consider these suggestions:

- Have a friend or parent help you.

- Begin work on an easier ritual.

- Work on the ritual only part of the day.

- Try simply disrupting the rituals (see Activity 26) for a few days, then try resisting them again.

# beating your stuck thoughts with exposure 30

## for you to know

Stuck thoughts try to convince you that you need to fear things that are not dangerous. Avoiding the feared things makes the stuck thought worse. Learning to expose yourself to what you fear empowers you to overcome that fear.

Did anyone ever try to get you to eat a food you thought you wouldn't like? You might have reluctantly tried a bite. But you expected it to be bad, so it probably didn't taste good the first time. If you kept at it, gradually—after trying a few times—you might actually have started to like it. You had to overcome two problems: you were negative about it to start with and then you had to get familiar with the new taste.

This is a good comparison for what has to happen to overcome the fears associated with stuck thoughts and rituals. Even though people tell you not to fear these things, your OCD makes you think they're really dangerous, and so you'd rather avoid them than try to face them. But when you *do* face them a few times, the fear goes away and you gain freedom from your false fears. This is called exposure, and learning to do it is the last major tool in beating OCD.

# for you to do

Let's practice understanding exposure before you apply it to your situation.

Kevin's stuck thought is that he hurts people's feelings by his choice of words when he texts them. So he avoids texting his friends.

Why is Kevin afraid to text?

_____

What will Kevin have to do to expose himself to his feared object?

_____

How will Kevin probably feel when he does this the first few times?

_____

What advice would you give Kevin on how to handle his thoughts and feelings when he tries to expose himself to texting?

_____

How do you think Kevin will feel after he's exposed himself to the feared situation several times?

_____

Veronica gets really nervous if her family members don't sit at the same places at the dinner table and if the silverware is not arranged in a specific pattern. She knows there's no danger here; it just makes her feel uncomfortable.

What will Veronica have to do to expose herself to the situation she fears?

_____

How do you think Veronica will feel the first time she does that?

_____

What advice would you give Veronica on how to handle her thoughts and feelings when she exposes herself to this situation?

_____

_____

_____

And, of course, you know she'll feel much more at ease after she does it a few times!

# wrapping it up

What are your first thoughts and feelings about trying exposure on your fearful thoughts and situations?

_____

_____

_____

If you did the activities just before this one, you have already experienced hanging in with fearful feelings without giving in to rituals.

Do you think exposing yourself to your fearful thoughts and situations will be:

easier     harder     about the same

What steps might you take to prepare for this important step in your victory over OCD?

_____

_____

_____

## for you to know

People with OCD can fear places, things, situations, certain actions, or certain thoughts. You need to be aware of all the things you're avoiding so you can apply your exposure skills to all of them.

As they waited for class to begin, Juanita peered over Angela's shoulder and saw her homework.

"Angela!" she said. "Your writing is neater than the print on my computer. How do you make all your rows of words line up to be the exact same length? That must take you forever!"

Angela smiled but started thinking. She had been perfectionistic about the neatness of her homework for so long that she didn't even notice it. She had made great progress on some of her stuck thoughts and rituals but hadn't even thought about her discomfort with any of her writing being messy or out of balance. Angela decided this would be the next project for her exposure skills.

# for you to do

Sometimes nervous feelings lead you to avoid things so automatically that you aren't even aware you are doing it. Let's make a list of everything your anxious thoughts and feelings cause you to avoid. It might help to ask someone who knows you well if there are any you missed.

Particular items I avoid (things I think are dirty, pictures that might make me have violent thoughts, etc.)

_____

_____

Places I avoid (public restrooms, places I associate with bad luck, etc.)

_____

_____

Situations I avoid (messy homework, books in a different order, etc.)

_____

_____

Actions I avoid (saying certain words, wearing certain colors, etc.)

_____

_____

Thoughts I avoid (thinking of death, counting to any number except the number that goes with my ritual, etc.)

_____

_____

# wrapping it up

Which of your answers were hardest to think of: items, places, situations, actions, or thoughts?

_____

Which one of these do you think will be the hardest to expose yourself to?

_____

Which do you think will be the easiest?

_____

Can you think of any of these you have genuine reasons to avoid? (For example, if you think bad language is wrong, you actually *should* avoid bad language.)

_____

# 32 facing your fears in your imagination

## for you to know

Often it's easiest to start facing fearful situations in your imagination. Many times you'll that find the feared situation is only in your head.

It isn't unusual that at fourteen, Connor likes horror movies, yet every time a scene from one of the movies pops into his head, his OCD makes him think that he is a violent person and may do something bad. Connor knows the facts: just because he has seen some scary films doesn't mean he's a serial killer. Still, any thought about one of the movies really upsets him.

Connor had struggled with fearing germs before, and exposing himself to public restrooms helped him overcome it. But how can he apply this technique to a fear that is only in his head?

Connor figured it out. Instead of running from the thoughts, he thought about the movies on purpose, took deep breaths when he felt anxious, and told himself, "OCD will not beat me!" Sure enough, he soon felt better.

# for you to do

Exposing yourself to uncomfortable things in your mind is useful when, like Connor, you have a stuck thought about a fear that is only in your head. It can also help you build confidence for real-life situations by coping with minor discomfort caused by just thinking about them. Let's try.

Do you have a stuck thought that makes you afraid of thinking about or imagining a particular thing? _____ If so, what is the thing you fear? (For Connor, it would be becoming a violent person.)

_____

What is the thought that leads to the fear? (Connor feared thoughts about horror movies he's seen.)

_____

Mental exposure means thinking the thought on purpose while fighting the fear. How would you do that, based on skills you've already learned?

_____

_____

_____

Now, think through a lower level of anxiety caused by imagining a situation that you fear due to stuck thoughts. (For example, Connor might have imagined walking into a school bathroom when he was battling the stuck thought that going there would make him sick.) Learning to think it without getting as nervous prepares you to face the situation in real life.

Choose one of your real-life fears caused by stuck thoughts:

_____

List several ways you might imagine this situation that would cause different levels of anxiety, from most difficult to least. (Connor might just think about the school restroom and then get more nervous by imagining himself walking into it.)

1. _____

2. _____

3. _____

Using skills you've learned, write what you could think that would enable you to face this situation with less fear.

_____

_____

_____

_____

Now, try exposing yourself to the fearful thing in your mind while fighting the fear with the thought you just wrote.

# wrapping it up

Describe your experience trying to expose yourself to a thought you fear.

_____

_____

_____

If you're using several levels of imagining, move on up to the next once you make good progress on the easiest.

After you've tried exposure, what changes would you make in the strategy you used? (Remember, learning from experience is important in beating OCD.)

_____

_____

_____

How does completing this activity make you feel about facing real-life situations that make you nervous?

_____

_____

_____

# 33 ranking situations that make you nervous

## for you to know

To overcome OCD, you need to know not only the situations that you fear, but also all the similar situations—both real and in your thinking—that make you nervous. You will be more successful if you know which make you the most nervous and which aren't so bad. In exposure, you start with the less troublesome ones and work your way up.

Shandara, whom we'll be getting to know over the next few activities, feared having to throw up. She had decided the smell of food anywhere but home would make her sick at her stomach. She then got really nervous about throwing up. This was now so bad that she couldn't even go near the doors of the school cafeteria.

Shandara had learned that she needed to expose herself to her fearful situation, but how could she when she couldn't even get near the cafeteria? Not to be defeated, she thought hard and then realized she didn't have to start in the cafeteria. She thought about all the places and situations where she felt nervous or sick and decided that she'd start on something easy.

# for you to do

First, know how to rate your symptoms of nervousness on a scale of 1 to 10 (Activity 23 can help you do this.)

Choose one thing you avoid due to OCD, and think through all the parts of it that stir up nervousness. Shandara, for example, would think not just about the cafeteria but also about different places and situations in it. Then she'd think of places near the cafeteria that bothered her. Finally, she'd list other things that make her nervous, like talking to her friends about the cafeteria or just thinking about it (yes, include thinking about it, looking at pictures of it, and other ways it can bother you without your actually being there or doing it).

Now, actually go to each situation briefly (or do the action briefly) to see how nervous each makes you. For some you may just have to guess if it's too troubling to actually do them. Rank each on a scale of 1 to 10.

| Situation | Score |
|---|---|
|  |  |
|  |  |
|  |  |
|  |  |
|  |  |
|  |  |
|  |  |
|  |  |

# wrapping it up

Once you have a list of all the situations that you avoid because OCD makes you uncomfortable, and how much each bothers you on a scale of 1 to 10, the next step toward success is to rank order them like Shandara did.

Shandara's scale might look like this:

Eating with my friends in the cafeteria                                          HIGHEST

Sitting at the table with my friends in the cafeteria

Standing in the cafeteria

Standing outside the cafeteria door

Standing down the hall but can smell the food a little bit

Standing further down the hall but can't smell the food

Talking to my friends about the cafeteria

Just thinking about eating in the cafeteria                                      LOWEST

Got the idea? Now try this for one of the things you avoid.

_____  HIGHEST

_____

_____

_____

_____

_____

_____

_____  LOWEST

## for you to know

When you face your nervous situation, you'll need a plan to help you hang in there when you have nervous thoughts and feelings.

Shandara was determined to beat the OCD that kept her from having lunch with friends at school. She got tired of giving them excuses and finally came clean, explaining to them that she was afraid she'd throw up when she smelled and saw the cafeteria food. They promised to encourage her as she worked through her plan to gradually get closer to eating with them. But she knew it would take more than her friends' encouragement, so she made a plan for how she would cope with her nervous feelings and thoughts when they came.

# for you to do

Shandara had her bases covered, for you need to have three things to hang in there when you expose yourself to your nervous thought or situation you've chosen to work on.

First, many teens can use some accountability. Shandara chose one way: letting friends (or parents) know what you're doing so they can ask you how it's going. This approach is a little gentle pressure to get you through. The other way is to make yourself accountable to start on a certain day.

Which do you prefer? (*Circle one*)          friend or parent          self

When will you start your plan? Be specific and commit yourself to this choice.

Day _____ Time _____

Second, you need to have a plan for coping with anxious thoughts. Review your thinking skills from earlier in the book if you need to and write your plan here:

When I start my nervous thought that _____

_____

might happen, I will stop the thought, identify it as a lie, and argue back at it by saying

_____

_____

Third, there are those troubling feelings that come. What do you do with them? Identify them as the liars they are, too, sounding an alarm when there's no danger.

Write what you will say to yourself about them:

_____

_____

Then, talk back by calming yourself through deep breaths and saying, "Settle down, self. There's no danger."

# wrapping it up

Can you think of any other things you might do or say to yourself to help you cope with the nervous thoughts and feelings that may come when you expose yourself to your difficult situation?

_____

_____

Do you have any songs, poems, or prayers that help you get psyched up that might be useful here as well?

_____

_____

You might put this all on a reminder card to carry with you.

| My Exposure Plan |
| --- |
| I am accountable to _____ |
| I'll battle thoughts with the following steps: |
| 1. _____ |
| 2. _____ |
| 3. _____ |
| And I'll battle feelings with these strategies: |
| 1. _____ |
| 2. _____ |
| 3. _____ |
| And my other weapon is:_____ |

# 35 exposing yourself

## for you to know

Overcoming situations you fear because of stuck thoughts takes letting yourself be exposed to them until your nervousness eases up. The key is beginning with less stressful situations and working your way up.

Shandara had worked hard to prepare to face her fears of the school lunchroom. She knew in her heart that the food there wasn't what made her sick at her stomach; it was the nervousness caused by her OCD. She had a plan: to take deep breaths and remind herself of the fun she was missing talking with her friends during lunch whenever the lie of OCD made her think there was danger at lunch. She was ready.

Monday came, and she was working through her plan. She even opened the cafeteria door. But then the combination of nervousness and nausea sent her back down the hallway to safety. Too much too fast: Shandara needed a more gradual plan.

If Shandara can learn to manage her anxious feelings one step at a time, she can work her way to success at having lunch with her friends.

# for you to do

Here's a checklist to make sure you're ready to expose yourself to a situation that makes you nervous.

- ☐ You know how to rank your nervous feelings as they occur from 1 (mild) to 10 (severe).

- ☐ You have listed situations that make you nervous, starting with mental situations that cause mild distress and continuing up to the real situation itself.

- ☐ You have a plan for deep breathing and talking back to your anxious feelings, including being convinced that the fear isn't real.

And let's add one more to help motivate you.

- ☐ You have set up a little reward for yourself for each step you pass, and a big one for when you reach the top:

My rewards: _____

Great. Now that you're ready, here's the idea. Start with the lowest fear. Imagine it or put yourself in that situation. What is your rating of discomfort? _____

If it's 3 or less, move on up to the next one and so forth until you have at least a 4.

Now stay with the fear and use your skills until you can get it down to a 2. Take as much practice as you need. When you succeed, move up to the next step in your list. Use your skills until this drops down to a 2. Got the idea? Keep going until you get all the way up your list. Take your time, but this is the key to beating OCD.

# wrapping it up

After you've worked on this plan for a few days, answer the following questions.

What changes did you make in your plan as you went along?

_____

_____

_____

Which step was the hardest so far?

_____

If you did get stuck on a step, what did you do?

_____

_____

(Suggestions include changing what you say to yourself, getting someone to help, adding a little step between where you are and the one you're stuck on, or changing rewards.)

If you are making progress, describe how it feels:

_____

_____

If parents or friends know you're working on this, share your success with them.

# doing what you fear 36
## on purpose

---

## for you to know

One of the best ways to prove to yourself that you've overcome stuck thoughts and rituals is to intentionally do the thing they worried you about.

---

Camille probably checked to see if she unplugged her hairdryer ten times before she could get out the door. She didn't want to be responsible for burning down the house or something. Her checking continued even though her parents convinced her that many things are plugged in all day and don't cause fires.

When trying to talk herself out of worrying about it failed, Camille was ready for drastic action. She left her hairdryer plugged in on purpose. It was sort of funny that she actually didn't worry as much because she now *knew* it was plugged in. She was nervous off and on during the day at school, but she wasn't surprised to pull into her driveway that afternoon to see her house still standing. She knew her need to check her hairdryer would be less of a problem from now on.

# for you to do

Lots of teens will find it a great idea to actually have permission to disobey—not their parents, but their OCD. Like them, you don't have to do what it says! Many kinds of OCD problems can be "disobeyed," like Camille did:

- If you fear germs on a sink, you can make yourself touch the sink.

- If you fear driving because you worry that you'll do something wrong, you can go for a drive—provided you have your license!

- If you get nervous when your backpack is messy, you can wad up a couple of papers and toss them in.

- If you are anxious that you'll say something that isn't perfectly accurate, you can say something you know isn't precise.

What problem caused by OCD do you have that you could defy by doing it on purpose?

_____

What will you need to do to disobey it?

_____

What skills that you've learned can help you defy the thing you're avoiding?

_____

_____

_____

Now give it a go.

# wrapping it up

What were you thinking when it was about time to disobey your OCD?

_____

_____

Did defying your OCD make you more or less nervous than you thought it would?

_____ Why? _____

_____

Is there anything you'll do differently next time you try this?

_____

Succeeding in disobeying your OCD felt as good as _____

_____

Sometimes new stuck thoughts and rituals try to work their way into your life. This skill can help run them off before they get a hold on you.

# 37 handling things that aren't "just right"

OCD often makes kids feel like they have to do things "just so" or have things "just right" to keep from feeling nervous. The skills you've learned can help with this, too.

Nolan obsessed about looking just right at school. His sister hassled him because he took so long in the bathroom in the mornings, making sure that his clothes and hair were perfect. He couldn't leave until he was confident that no one could fault his appearance. Still, he knew he was overdoing it, and he knew no one would stop being his friend if his hair wasn't just right.

Getting detention for being late yet again made Nolan determined to stop this behavior. He had come a long way in overcoming OCD, and this piece of it would be next to go down in defeat. The following morning, Nolan didn't even comb his hair after his shower and skipped a belt loop on purpose so that his outfit wasn't perfect. Sure a couple of his friends teased him—but not before Nolan joked about it himself. What a great feeling to be released from trying to look just right!

# for you to do

First, let's identify the things like this that bother you. These can include stuff like having to completely erase any mistakes on your paper, feeling you have to make 100 on every assignment and test, having to balance your desk so that there are a certain number of things on each side, and so on.

_____

_____

_____

Now think about why you feel you have to have things "just so." Write it here:

_____

_____

Usually this behavior is to avoid an uncomfortable feeling similar to nervousness. Use your reasoning skills: is this a genuine fear or a false one? _____

What can you say to yourself when you think or feel this way?

_____

_____

How might you use your skills at facing your fears and exposing yourself to them to fight acting this way, based on what you have learned so far?

_____

_____

_____

# wrapping it up

Some people whose OCD makes them sensitive to things being "just so" get frustrated or irritated with others who don't do things the way they want them to.

From what you know about OCD, why do think this might be?

_____

_____

What advice would you give to a person who struggles with this problem?

_____

_____

Do you think this might apply to you? _____ Why or why not?

_____

_____

How might the skills you practiced in this activity help when others don't do things just the way you want them to?

_____

_____

## for you to know

To keep strong against stuck thoughts and rituals, it is helpful to review what you've learned.

Lindsay was feeling pretty good about the progress she'd made on her OCD. She had texted her cousin Danielle about her fight with stuck thoughts and rituals, but when they got to see each other at the family reunion, Danielle wanted to hear the whole story.

Lindsay was more than happy to oblige her cousin. As she talked, Lindsay realized how far she had come—even more than she had realized before. She also noticed that a couple of the skills she had learned had slipped her mind. She was glad to realize this, because she knew her OCD could strike back if she gave it a chance.

# for you to do

Since you may not have a cousin asking you to tell the story, imagine a newspaper editor hears of your progress and wants you to write a brief story. The editor asks you to cover a little about what OCD is, what you did to get better, and what advice you might give to other teens who have it. You might look back over the activities you've done before you write this, and try to be detailed.

_____

_____

_____

_____

_____

_____

_____

_____

_____

_____

_____

_____

_____

_____

_____

_____

# wrapping it up

In doing this activity, did you notice any important skills that had slipped your mind? If so, which ones?

_____

_____

_____

What do you think is the biggest difference in your life now that your OCD is more under control?

_____

_____

_____

What do you think you need to do to keep fighting your OCD to finish it off and to keep it out of your way?

_____

_____

_____

# 39 back in the game

## for you to know

OCD is a bit naughty and will often try to sneak up and take over your life again. Realizing how far you have come can help you stay strong and resist new stuck thoughts and rituals.

As Jamaal, whom we met back in Activity 2, sat in class waiting for the teacher to begin, he remembered last semester when he was about ready to drop out of school because his ritual of straightening everything got him teased by his friends so much. Now he enjoyed being in class and could even look at a messy stack of papers without feeling an urge to straighten them. He realized he had probably been depressed before. But now, with his thoughts being his own and not the nagging of OCD, he was happier than he'd been in a while. School was still hard, but he was happy to be there.

# for you to do

Think back to when you began this program (review Activities 2 and 3 if you did them). For each area, tell how your OCD affected your life then. What has changed in these areas, if anything, now that OCD is less in control of your life?

|  | Then | Now |
|---|---|---|
| Your happiness | | |
| Your social life | | |
| Your free time | | |
| Your relationships with your family members | | |
| Your feelings about yourself | | |

# wrapping it up

Which area of change surprises you most? _____

Why?_____

_____

How has your improvement affected your school work and performance?

_____

_____

What are you doing with your freedom that you couldn't do before?

_____

_____

# the story of your success 40

## for you to know

Knowing how far you've come, and planning for the future, will help keep you free from OCD.

Reese had been pretty much free from stuck thoughts and rituals for months now, but suddenly she found herself afraid she'd say something bad about someone accidentally and saying a ritual prayer to ease her anxiety.

"Not going there!" she said to herself. She thought back on how miserable she'd been when she let her OCD talk to her instead of her talking to her OCD. She pulled out her review sheet where she'd written down her keys to success, and she resolved to fight back from the start. As she expected, her OCD backed off and left her alone once again. What a great feeling to know she had tamed an animal like OCD!

# for you to do

Reese was wise to have a brief summary of what she'd learned ready in case her thoughts came back.

Make a summary sheet of the keys to your success so you have it ready for future reference. It is a good idea to review these keys from time to time, even before OCD tries to get back in.

---

### REMINDER OF MY KEYS TO SUCCESS

When I notice myself thinking a stuck thought, I know I have to fight it and treat it as the lie that it is. The best ways to do that are:

1. _____

2. _____

3. _____

When I feel nervous if I don't do a ritual, I must resist the ritual. The best ways for me to do that are:

1. _____

2. _____

3. _____

When I feel nervous, I can replace my rituals by:

1. _____

2. _____

3. _____

---

# wrapping it up

From what you've learned working on your OCD, what might be a few situations where you think your OCD might sneak up on you again?

1. _____

2. _____

3. _____

What is your plan for staying alert in those situations?

_____

_____

_____

Who could you ask to tell you if he or she notices any signs of stuck thoughts and rituals in your behavior? _____

Set a few dates to review the sheet you just made to help prevent OCD from coming back.

One month from today:        _____

Three months from today:     _____

Six months from today:       _____

Commit yourself to these reviews. Put them on a calendar or in reminders on your cell phone. These are "booster shots" to maintain your gains.

*Here's wishing you a wonderful life free from OCD!*

**Timothy A. Sisemore, Ph.D.**, is professor of counseling and psychology at Richmont Graduate University in Chattanooga, TN, and maintains a private practice in clinical psychology. He specializes in treating anxiety disorders in children and adolescents. Sisemore is author of several books, including *I Bet I Won't Fret*.